I'll Push, You Pull

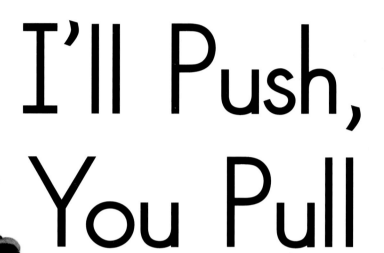

Paul Humphrey

Illustrated by
Katy Sleight

STECK-VAUGHN
C O M P A N Y
ELEMENTARY • SECONDARY • ADULT • LIBRARY

4

I'll Push, You Pull

Acknowledgments
Executive Editor: Diane Sharpe
Supervising Editor: Stephanie Muller
Design Manager: Sharon Golden
Page Design: Simon Balley Design Associates
Photography: Action Plus: pages 11, 18, 19; Bruce Coleman:
cover (both); Eye Ubiquitous: page 15; Image Bank: pages 13,
20, 21; Alex Ramsay: pages 9, 17; ZEFA: page 12.

ISBN 0-8114-3702-7

I'll push and you pull.

5

8

He pulls the thread.

9

I push the stroller.

10

The rowers pull the oars.

What else pushes?

The snow plow pushes the snow off the road.

What else pulls?

The engine pulls the train.

13

I pull on my boots.

14

He pushes down on the pedals.

I pull up
the weeds.

16

He pushes the wheelbarrow.

The man lifts the weights.

18

Then he pushes them into the air.

The tractor pulls the plow.

The bulldozer pushes the rocks.

21

I push the sled.

We all ride down the hill!

Then we have to pull the sled up
the hill again.

24

We all push the car.

25

We all pull in tug-of-war.

26

We all fall over!

28

Which things push?
Which things pull?
Which things can push and pull?